IMAGES
of England

MATLOCK
AND
MATLOCK BATH

Compiled by
Julie Bunting

TEMPUS

First published 2002
Copyright © Julie Bunting, 2002

Tempus Publishing Limited
The Mill, Brimscombe Port,
Stroud, Gloucestershire, GL5 2QG

ISBN 0 7524 2455 6

Typesetting and origination by
Tempus Publishing Limited
Printed in Great Britain by
Midway Colour Print, Wiltshire

One of the greatest Victorian undertakings in Derbyshire was Matlock's cable car tramway. Here is the reason for its existence: the formidably steep Bank Road, pictured in 1918. Not only did Matlock boast the first single-line cable tramway in Europe, but at its opening in March 1893 it was the steepest in the world, with an average gradient of $1:5\frac{1}{2}$ over its $\frac{5}{8}$-mile length.

Contents

Reserve your Holiday

FOR THE

GREAT TEMPERANCE TRIP

TO

MATLOCK.

THE

Doncaster Temperance Society,

HAVE MADE ARRANGEMENTS WITH THE

Midland Railway Company

FOR A

CHEAP DAY TRIP

TO

MATLOCK

AND

ROWSLEY,
On JUNE 26th, 1866.

FARES—First Class ·················· 5s. 0d.
          Covered Carriages ···· 2s. 6d.
Children under Twelve years of age, half fare,
Including FREE ADMISSION to the "Heights of
Abraham," "Rutland Cavern" and "Prospect Tower."

WEEKLY PAYMENTS towards the purchase
of Tickets, &c., can be received by Mr. J. Brooks, Spring
Gardens; Mr. R. Porter, Scot Lane; Mr. Snelling, Union
Street; Mr. Tretheway, Fitzwilliam Street; Mr. Crossley,
French-gate; Mr. Spencer, Stationer, St. Sepulchre-gate;
Mr. Smith, Bridge Street; Mr. Tuxworth, James Street;
and by the Printer.

N.B. An Early application for tickets is respectfully
requested.

H. SCOTT, GENERAL PRINTER, DONCASTER.

On 1 June 1849, the Midland Railway opened the line from Ambergate to Rowsley, later extended to Manchester. Matlock station became the destination of thousands of travellers, from excursionists to hydro visitors, who alighted from the London express with contingents of servants. This excursion bill was a little something to tempt the Temperance day tripper. (Doncaster Museum and Art Gallery)

6

Introduction

Nature has been generous to the Peak District and nowhere more so than Matlock and Matlock Bath. Even the disused stone quarries and lead workings blend into the scenery and although scars from quarrying exclude the scenic Matlocks from the Peak District National Park, there is little to detract from its overall setting.

The existence of lead, and a little silver, was discovered by the Romans, who may or may not have known of the thermal waters but, for once, did not exploit them, as happened further north at Buxton. The earliest recorded use of Matlock Bath's warm waters for relief dates from the end of the seventeenth century, but only on a local scale until a bath house, the famous Old Bath, was built on a terrace below the Heights of Jacob. The Old Bath was superseded by the magnificent Royal Hotel.

Until the scattered village of Matlock Bath achieved fame as a spa, it was known simply as Matlock, while present-day Matlock was an insignificant cold-water neighbour, biding its time until the hydropathic boom. Meanwhile, the warm springs of the Derwent gorge, drunk with milk or cream, were considered 'efficacious in glandular affections, rheumatism, biliary obstruction, incipient consumption and in all complaints arising from relaxation of the muscular fibres'.

The rich and famous discovered Matlock Bath and made the place fashionable. Its beauty was celebrated by Defoe, Sir Walter Scott, Eliza Cook and Lord Byron, whose doomed acquaintance with Mary Chaworth began at the Old Bath. Byron made a favourable comparison between the local scenery and parts of Switzerland, while Mary Shelley makes a similar point in Frankenstein: 'The country in the neighbourhood of this village [Matlock Bath] resembled, to a greater degree, the scenery of Switzerland; but everything is on a lower scale, and the green hills want the crown of distant white Alps ... We visited the wondrous cave, and the cabinets of natural history, where the curiosities are disposed in the same manner as in the collections at Servox and Chamounix'.

Amongst other illustrious nineteenth-century visitors were the Archdukes John and Louis of Austria; Duke Nicholas (later Emperor) of Russia; Imperial Grand Duke Michael of Russia; Princess (future Queen) Victoria with her 'august mother', the Duchess of Kent; Dowager Queen Adelaide; Emperor Dom Pedro II of Brazil and his Empress; and Princess (later Queen) Mary.

The village was by now a leading resort, with a lively season lasting from spring to late autumn. At times when continental tours were impracticable, generally when a war was being conducted somewhere in Europe, well-to-do visitors came to stay in Matlock Bath for several months at a time. This exclusive way of life changed considerably with the arrival of the railway, when the number of short-term and day visitors to Matlock Bath soared.

A New Era

Meanwhile, a new era had dawned in health care with the introduction to England of hydropathy. Whereas the spas of Matlock Bath and Buxton utilized thermal springs for internal consumption, hydropathy was the use of water to apply external hot or cold treatments to specific parts of the body. One man who had recovered his health following a (very cold) water cure, after believing himself beyond help, was John Smedley, owner of the textile factory which still bears his name at Lea Mills. Smedley conceived an innovative Mild Water Cure which he tried out first on his employees, with the result that he was encouraged to turn his pioneering zeal towards the pure waters of Matlock.

Success was immediate, and its repercussions changed the face of Matlock for ever. Smedley's own imposing hydro was soon to be joined by imitators but, more importantly, the small town was transformed as its individual settlements – the old town, Matlock Green, Matlock Bank, Matlock Bridge and Matlock Dale – expanded to form a cohesive and vibrant market town. Between 1861 and 1881, there was an increase in population of almost forty per cent.

The growing number of hydros, new houses, shops and public buildings created jobs and utilized local stone, often both together. Properties were built to impress with balconies, fluted columns, balustrades, shapely pinnacles and turrets, stylish windows and curved glass panes which would cost a fortune today. Local gritstone also found a wider market. Not only was it noted for its ability to survive 'the particularly disintegrating effect of the London atmosphere' but its hardness actually improved when exposed to the air. In fact HM Office of Works considered stone from Drabble's quarries to be so superior as to 'afford maximum protection to public documents from fire and any manner of risks'.

Stone quarried from around Matlock built a new savings bank in the capital, theatres in the West End, the Savoy Hotel, the Hotel Metropole near Charing Cross, and many railway bridges, canals and post offices across the country. It went into major constructions in the Midlands, including the building of Derby Royal Infirmary, renovations to Nottingham Castle and, on the local scene, the Whitworth Hospital at Darley Dale.

The coming of the railway had set the seal on Matlock's commercial success and the station was a scene of constant activity. A number of coal and stone depots operated in the goods yard, while horse-drawn drugs, and later steam wagons, delivered pulp stones for export to Scandinavian paper mills, grindstones for sharpening tools in manufacturing industries and, as mentioned, building stone. Passenger traffic kept the platform staff bustling, with several express trains a day in each direction stopping at the station. Some hydros sent vehicles to meet their guests at the station, though with the advent of the motor car, several taxi firms plied long hours between the station and smaller establishments, particularly hotels and guesthouses.

It seems fitting that the town's greatest hydro, Smedley's, was last to close, almost half a century ago. But Matlock was not about to fade quietly into its past. The palatial building on the Bank was chosen as the new headquarters of Derbyshire County Council and, in spite of its popular local nickname (The Kremlin), is now settling into its official up-to-date title of County Hall, quite at home in this most scenic and historic Derbyshire town.

Julie Bunting
November 2001

Glenorchy House was demolished half a century ago, during improvements to the A6 through Matlock Bath. The house was originally the residence of Samuel Need, manager to Sir Richard Arkwright at nearby Masson Mill. In 1785, Lady Glenorchy, a wealthy religious revivalist, purchased the property, onto which she built and endowed a chapel for independent worship.

Matlock

One

Water, Water Everywhere

Bridges all the way down the flood-prone Derwent have, at various times, been swept away, Matlock bridge being a rare exception. All the same, the river regularly burst its banks on its way through Matlock, sometimes several times a year, and major roads in the town centre and at Matlock Green could be cut off by up to 6ft of water. This was the bleak scene outside shops on Bakewell Road in 1907. The undeveloped area with the trees later became the bus station and open market, but now lies beneath a supermarket complex.

From the start of the new millennium, stylish new road signs in green and gold have welcomed walkers, cyclists and drivers to Matlock – Picturesque Spa Town. The wording differs slightly on the various signs; this one stands on Matlock Moor beside the Chesterfield road, shortly before the views open up to give a sweeping vista of hills and dales.

Allen Hill Spa, at the foot of the Dimple, once had a reputation for easing eye complaints. Leaving a brownish-yellow deposit, the water looks most unappetizing but, in the 1890s, it was acclaimed as second to none in the country and reckoned to be well worthy of a pump room surrounded by gardens and promenades – it does at least have a small garden.

Matlock's medieval bridge over the Derwent, before it was widened in 1903/4. Pedestrians had neither footpaths nor quoins to squeeze into when traffic passed by. The large house surrounded by trees, now a bank, was then a private residence and had earlier been a boarding school for young ladies. The railway station can be seen to the far right.

Although the streets of Matlock were well paved, drained and cleaned, the ancient narrow bridge was a real bottleneck and subject to immense weights from horse-drawn drugs transporting quarried stone to the station. In 1903, sentiment was sacrificed to progress and work commenced on widening the old bridge on the upstream side.

For nearly forty years, the Derwent has hosted a regular Boxing Day spectacle, drawing large crowds of spectators to the annual raft races. And anything goes, as long as it floats. It has been known for 200 precarious-looking craft to set off from the official start at Cawdor Quarry with another hundred or so joining in further downriver.

In many ways, horse-drawn traffic coped better with the all-too-regular floods than did later forms of transport. As far as the tramway was concerned, everything came to a halt as soon as the underground wheels of the cable system were submerged, and the lower section never escaped a flooding. Hence, this early twentieth-century tram is almost certainly immobilized.

December 1965, and this time, viewed from the Crown Hotel, the van replaces the tram. If the driver could just make it round the bend onto the lower slopes of Bank Road, dry land lay ahead. The mock-Tudor buildings were occupied by Burgon's and, furthest left, by Derbyshire Times Newspapers.

Meanwhile, this was the scene in the *Matlock Mercury* print room, further along Bakewell Road. Newspaper staff stand thigh-deep in cold, dirty water, as they make up pages for the imminent edition. Against all odds, they beat the deadline and the Mercury came out on time. From left to right: Neville Boulton, Terry Stone, Jack Mudway, Adrian Duggins.

The floods of 1931 were notorious for damage and for the numbers of people rescued by rowing boat. Well wrapped-up bystanders examine the damage caused to Burgon's plate-glass window, apparently by a telegraph pole, though some witnesses said the missile was a large metal tank which had launched itself out of Billy Twigg's scrap yard.

Burgon's own brands went under the name of Numnah and used the logo of a black elephant, seen cast in relief on the rear wall of the store. In digging out the foundations to build Burgon's, a human skeleton was found. An inquiry concluded that it was possibly that of a felon hanged at the adjoining cross roads.

Matlock Lido was opened in June 1938 by Carnival Queen Lilian Knowles, who still lives locally and recalls that for the event, she and her retinue wore woollen bathing suits from the Smedley factory at nearby Lea Bridge. This 1950s scene, with lots of personal bathing space, indicates a cool day; attendances always reflected the barometer.

The Lido under 2in of ice on a winter's morning in January 1968. Seen breaking the ice, is Lido superintendent Jack Soppitt, held in great affection by the many hundreds of local people that he taught to swim as children. Still known to many as the Lido, the swimming pool is now under a glass roof.

16

Two
The Mild Water Cure

The world-famous Smedley's Hydropathic Establishment at the height of its success. The central tower and huge extension to its right were additions of the 1880s. Smedley's name appears on the castellated section. From modest beginnings, his hydro had gone from strength to strength, until he was personally supervising an average 2,000 patients per year alone. The original list of almost 300 water treatments ranged from the ascending douche (hot, cold and under pressure!) to immersion, needle, galvanic or steambox baths and the Neckrozoon massage! The advent of electricity in 1888 brought new 'electro' treatments onto the agenda. The grand interior of the hydro, its magnificent landscaped grounds and spectacular views, set it apart from the competition. There was even an Artist's Photographic Studio in the grounds, with a 'by appointment' relationship with the proprietors. Here, the distinguished visitor could sit for a carte de visite or even an impressive life-sized photographic portrait.

John Smedley (1803-1874), without whom Matlock would be so different today. Derbyshire County Council would almost certainly not have set up headquarters here and hundreds of other properties, Riber Castle included, would never have been built. Smedley, a mill owner, regained his health after visiting a Yorkshire spa in 1847, and was motivated to pioneer his own Mild Water Cure. The little market town of Matlock was transformed by his meteoric success.

Smedley had launched his innovative water cure, free of charge, upon his workforce at Lea Mills, with such encouraging results that he then took over a small hydro on Matlock Bank. This steep, sparsely populated hillside had the advantage of an abundant supply of pure water from Matlock Moor, the prerequisite for Smedley's first massive expansion of 1868, the subject of this engraving.

RULES AND REGULATIONS
MR. SMEDLEY'S
HYDROPATHIC ESTABLISHMENT
NEAR MATLOCK BRIDGE STATION, DERBYSHIRE.

MEALS.

BREAKFAST, 8.30 a.m. DINNER, 2.0 p.m. TEA, 6.30 p.m.
Sundays.— BREAKFAST, 8.30 a.m. DINNER, 1.0 p.m. TEA, 5.0 p.m
SUPPER *(for those who require it)* : Bread, Butter, Milk, and Water. will be on
the Table in the Dining Saloon after Prayers.

RELIGIOUS SERVICES.
(ATTENDANCE ENTIRELY OPTIONAL.)

FAMILY WORSHIP every Morning after Breakfast, and in the Evening at 9.0
PUBLIC WORSHIP in the CHAPEL every SUNDAY, as follows :—
Morning, 10.30 ; Evening, 6.30. *Wednesday* Evenings, at 7.30.

For the Maintenance of Due Decorum, the following Fines have been Established by the Recreation Committee :—

	s.	d.		s.	d.
Any person who shall come to meals after a blessing has been asked ...	0	1	the piano or games during the twenty minutes of rest after the Bible reading at dinner-time	0	1
Any allusion to " treatment" during meals	0	1	Any gentleman entering the ladies' sitting-room	10	6
The mention of the word " crisis," or any synonymous word during meals	0	2.	Any gentleman entering the ladies' bath-room	10	6
Reading, writing, working or playing					

Whoever tempts another to break any of these rules to pay the fine themselves.

CONSULTING DAYS.
SUMMER.—Mondays, Wednesdays, and Fridays.
WINTER.—Mondays and Thursdays.

Patients must apply to head bath-woman and head bath-man when Mr. and
Mrs. SMEDLEY are not in. A waiter in saloons constantly, to go on errands
and give information. ACCOUNTS issued every Wednesday ; attendance for
payment of same in the Drawing-room, from 2.30 to 5.0 p.m.

Steward—MR. JONAS BROWN. *Matron—MISS GIBBINS.*

Owing to the Delicate State of Health of some of the Patients, it is felt necessary for the future to adopt the following Rules ;—

CHILDREN under 14 years of age will not be allowed to go into the Drawing-
room, or allowed to be in the Saloon, except at Breakfast, Dinner, and Tea ;
their Bed-rooms, the Chapel (60 feet long, 30 feet wide), Covered Walk (200
feet), and Grounds, will be the only part of the Establishment for them to resort
to. The Chapel will be kept warmed all day when season requires, so that they
may be there as much as they like. INFANTS not admitted into the Establishment.

Mr. SMEDLEY hoped to have been able to invite Medical Practitioners to stay
in this Establishment and witness the treatment, but Patients *will* apply to them
on the subject of their health, and become uneasy as to the course prescribed
for them. Mr. SMEDLEY is in consequence obliged to come to the decision that
Practitioners can only come for the day to see the Establishment, or to see
Patients.

John Smedley regarded high moral standards and religious services as essential to his
undertaking – his wife, Caroline, was, after all, the daughter of a vicar. The couple imposed a
strict regime on their patients; a ban on dancing and alcohol was rigorously enforced and this
table of rules and regulations was in existence in 1862. Even leading others into temptation
attracted a fine!

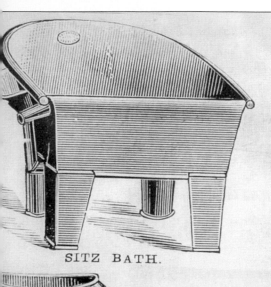
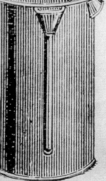

Smedley's good fortune rubbed off on businesses such as 'Tinker' Wright's, ironmongers on Smedley Street since at least 1881. Michael Wright had the initiative to move from Matlock Green and he found a ready market – both over-the-counter and mail order – for appliances and bandages, copper chest-warmers and the Patent Ascending Douche, of which he was 'manufacturer and sole stockist'.

The Ascending Douche in full force – and a patient quite taken by surprise. Tinker Wright also manufactured an equally uncomfortable-looking invention of Smedley's, the running sitz bath. With the appearance of a perforated chair, it 'produced good action of the bowels and healthily braced the nerves of the spine and brain'.

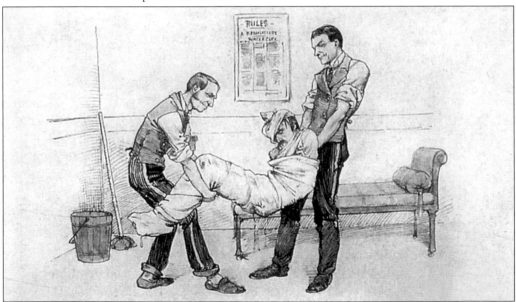

By the time of the wet sheet cure, our patient looks the worse for wear. Firmly cocooned in wet sheets, he has been thoroughly doused with water and will be laid out while the cold sheet warms up against his body, causing 'a general glow throughout the frame'; supposedly a good tonic for a fatigued system.

While curious locals dawdled past liveried footmen at the grand main entrance, perhaps to catch the arrival of a VIP, the gardens and grounds of the hydro were a haven of genteel social activity. Little is known about this intriguing photograph, but the monkey seems to have escaped from its cage. And the elderly gentleman looks quite oblivious.

All hydros had their share of valetudinarian guests with the means to indulge a degree of high-class hypochondria. They expected a refined social life between 'treatments', so establishments vied to offer inducements from heated garages and all delicacies of table to bagatelle, chess, elocutionary entertainment and, as we see here, whist.

This sequence of behind-the-scenes activities was recorded at Smedley's around 1900. The hydro's recent annual report had revealed that income for 1888/89, at £36,000, was the highest in its half-century history. A year of 'unparalleled prosperity' had seen the purchase of a ten-acre farm at Farley to supply the hydro with fresh milk, eggs, poultry and farm produce.

Many hundreds of local people took up jobs at Smedley's and worked here until they retired. Seasonal workers helped to keep operations running smoothly, as did a number of ex-military men – and if the stern bearing of the chap on the left is anything to go by, he may have been one of them.

Not one of the more hectic days in the kitchens. By comparison, Smedley's Hydro was full to capacity over Christmas 1899, with a further 170 hopeful guests turned away. The magnificent Corinthian Dining Hall seated over 300, with a menu offering such delights as oysters, clear turtle soup, haunch of venison or roast goose.

The post room, after distribution of the latest batch of incoming mail, leaving just a couple of newspapers in the 200-plus pigeon holes. A book of telegram forms hangs nearby. The weighing of outgoing mail is in progress, note the balance scales on the counter, and two very smart, but very young, post boys barely have time to turn to the camera.

John Smedley did not hold onto his monopoly for long. Others came to tap into his supply – of both the local water and the continuous stream of patients. At least thirty establishments came into being. Lilybank, formerly Dalefield and seen here around 1935, existed as a hydro until 1950. After many years as a preparatory school, Lilybank is now a residential home.

Nothing seems out of the ordinary here, but this was one of the hugely popular staff balls held at Lilybank Hydro between the wars. Once a year the tables were turned, when it was the clients who provided an apparently smiling service to members of staff and their guests, a tradition also observed at Smedley's.

The visitors' unaccustomed subservience is coming to an end, as the staff enjoy a final taste of – and perhaps a toast to – the way the other half lives. Practically all hydro servants and medical attendants worked seven days a week and this Lilybank contingent is clearly relishing its special night out.

Several hydros were taken over for military use during both World Wars. The weekend that war was declared in 1939, the owners of Oldham House Hydro were away and they returned on the Monday to find the building unceremoniously emptied of its residents and commandeered for imminent use as an RAF hospital. The property later became part of a teacher training college.

Bank House Hydro, later Wyvern House Hydro, is best remembered as the Ernest Bailey Grammar School, named after its founder. Until 'Bailey's' opened in 1924, most of those children who obtained scholarships had to travel to Belper or Bakewell. The school closed in 1982 and is now Derbyshire Record Office.

A wealthy mill owner and great benefactor to the town, Ernest Bailey also maintained St Andrew's House on Matlock Cliff as an orphanage for the Church of England Waifs' and Strays' Society. This 1981 photograph shows the proximity of the twin-gabled St Andrew's House to Bailey's former flour mill, where work was found for many of the orphans after they left school.

The magnificently sited Rockside was another major hydro, just within reach of the cable tramway. In the First World War it became an auxiliary hospital for wounded servicemen, and, in the Second World War, an RAF psychiatric hospital for air-crew suffering combat fatigue. In later years, as Rockside Hall, the building became part of the teacher training college.

After the death of John Smedley, his widow and staunch helpmate, Caroline, founded in his memory the Smedley Memorial Hydropathic Hospital on Bank Road. The hospital practised their shared philanthropic ideal of bringing free treatment to the needy. Later used as a convalescent hospital, the property finally relinquished medical use when it took on its present role as a youth hostel.

Three
Wartime

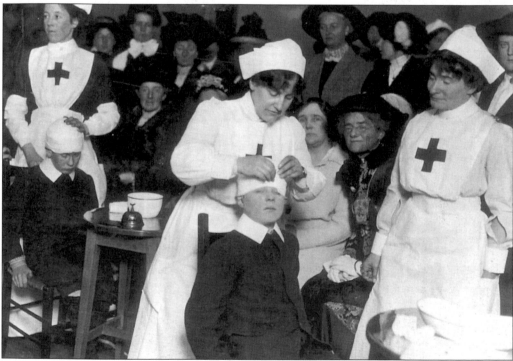

A public demonstration by Red Cross nurses at Wirksworth in March 1914. The previous year, the Derbyshire branch of the Red Cross had collected and supplied comforts for sick and wounded soldiers in the Balkan war. During the First World War, working parties made clothing and dressings, and by the end of hostilities, 1 million garments and bandages had passed through the County Clearing House. Derbyshire Red Cross also provided a motorized soup kitchen for use at the front, with sufficient money to maintain it. Care of sick and wounded ex-servicemen and POWs continued in peacetime, backed with the loan of medical equipment. The Red Cross also collected and distributed clothing for miners' families during the 1920s depression and gave sterling support to struggling farmers. All too soon, the organization was again proving its worth with the outbreak of the Second World War.

At the end of the nineteenth century, musketry officials from the War Office approved adoption of the latest targets at Cuckoostone shooting range, as it was now suitable for the new rifle. A number of companies and battalions put in regular practice at Cuckoostone, as did members of Matlock and District Rifle Club, seen here in 1910.

According to the reverse of this photograph, these three unnamed 'Matlock Patriots' were the first local men to enlist for the First World War. They are apparently waiting at the railway station, about to leave home for military training camps. Many more would follow their example, and the Matlock area was to lose 179 men in the war.

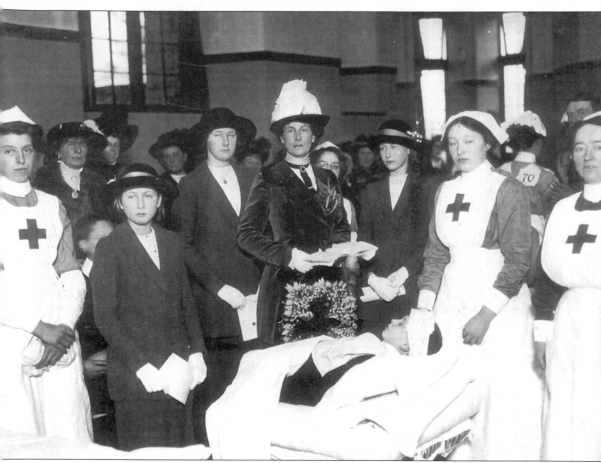

Evelyn, Duchess of Devonshire, became president of the Derbyshire branch of the British Red Cross Society at its formation in 1909. Uniquely at the time, the Duchess encouraged supporters who could give practical rather than financial help, setting up voluntary aid detachments in townships including Matlock. Here, the Duchess and her daughters, the Ladies Blanche, Dorothy and Rachel Cavendish, preside over a nursing and first aid competition held at Rockside Hydro in January 1914.

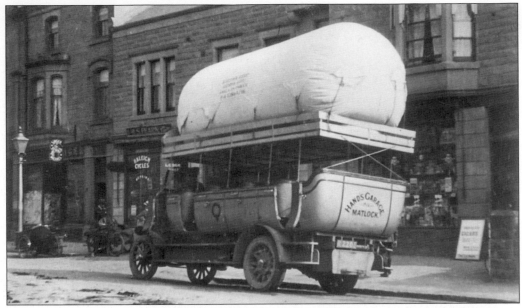

With the inevitable petrol shortages of the First World War, this motor bus belonging to Hand's Garage was one of many larger vehicles which trundled around Britain with ungainly gas bags anchored to their roofs. This photograph of around 1917 was taken by W. Rex Kirkby of Westcliff-on-Sea, a keen traveller and photographer.

Alice Brookhouse was the town's first woman taxi driver. Her opportunity came about during the First World War, when there were more important roles for the menfolk than driving taxis. After the war, Alice married a New Zealand soldier and returned with him to his native country, from where she maintained links with Matlock until at least the 1980s.

These Victory celebrations took place in front of the houses on Quarry Lane in 1919 and demonstrate the strong sense of community which united the often large families of Matlock Moor, where nearly all the men earned their living in either farming or quarrying.

Matlock War Memorial stands on the summit of Pic Tor, a popular 360-degree viewpoint visible from the various descents into town. The memorial was constructed of Lumshill stone by Matlock builders Wildgoose and Sons Ltd. These workmen are securing the cross in early December 1922. The wooden board at the base has yet to be replaced with the inscribed memorial tablets.

William Smith saw action in the First World War and is seen here in the Second. As leader of a mounted platoon of the Home Guard, he conducted nocturnal horseback patrols through the local hills. By day, he and his wife made the daily thirty-five mile round trip to Eyam, where he owned a mine being worked for spar, by horse and trap.

During the Second World War, with the very real fear of the enemy reaching the Midlands, a specially trained covert civilian unit, Ground Station Zero, came into being. One of its top secret wireless stations was installed in Tailor Toplis's shop at 135 Smedley Street, the aerial fixed out of sight on the chimney pot. A pistol, ammunition and hand grenade were kept beside the wireless set. Not a whisper of all this reached the unwitting neighbours until many years after the war.

Four

On the Map

As Matlock rose in importance, the late Victorian Crown Hotel was built to replace an earlier establishment of the same name which had been located near the present bus station. The new Crown was arguably the best hotel in the town centre and certainly a vast improvement on its predecessor, a common lodging house with a low reputation. That one has gone down in legend for the class of its clientele, which included travelling men who brought their monkeys and dancing bears. Visiting bears were kept in pens in the old Crown cellars. Barely visible on this early twentieth-century photograph, is a carved crown on the corner of the building, just above the eye-level of the hundreds of shoppers who now bustle round this corner every day.

'I was bound, like a child, by some magical story;
Forgetting the "South" and "Ionian Vales":
And felt that dear England had Temples of Glory,
Where any might worship, in Derbyshire Dales.'

(Eliza Cook)

Buildings to the right of this Edwardian scene, leading towards Kirkham's shoe shop – now Dakin's newsagent – are still familiar, but those opposite were demolished in 1926/27. A barber's pole identifies Philip's hairdressers, then came Margerrison's outfitters, later Gessy's stationers, and Orme and Co., grocers. Straight ahead is the first post office, which relocated to Bank Road in 1912.

Linking Crown Square and Matlock Green, Causeway Lane took its name from the early causeway of huge stone slabs that carried quarry and mill traffic across the low-lying water meadows. These carts are, in fact, splashing through several inches of water. Today, Alldays and Woolworth's stand on land which had to be drained and cleared of large beech trees.

Now the A6, the narrow road beside the Railway Inn used to separate it from Bateman's Park, owned by John Bateman, proprietor of the Railway Inn from the late nineteenth century. This photograph dates from his tenure. Circuses, menageries and wakes used to set up on Bateman's Park and an annual fair continued to be held on the site, long after it became a public car park.

The nineteenth-century boom in the local population brought the need for more schools and Matlock School Board was formed in August 1895. Two years later, a council school opened off Chesterfield Road for 250 mixed and 120 infants; these are pupils of 1912. Another number on the chalk board has clearly been altered to match the class.

This staff assembly from the same school in the late 1930s shows, from left to right, standing: Miss Reeve, Alan Prasher, Miss Ballington, W. College, Miss Henstock. Front row, seated: Miss Slater, Miss Austin, Mr Mills (headmaster), Miss Millington (Mrs Barber) and Miss Ellison. Widely known as the Board School, long after it became Matlock County Primary, it is now Castle View Primary School.

A small school had been open to the sons of Matlock inhabitants for some time before Matlock Town Endowed School was built in 1860. This was extended almost thirty years later to accommodate 250 pupils, although attendances were always far less. As Matlock Town Church of England Primary School, the building has recently been sold and converted to three dwellings.

All the children of Starkholmes must have been present for this photograph, taken on 22 June 1911, during celebrations for the Coronation of King George V and Queen Mary. The absence of adults may imply that a party had been laid on just for these youngsters, probably at their nearby school.

Nonconformist churches were well represented on Matlock Bank when work began on All Saints' church in 1882. An Anglican church had already been built a short distance away, but only for the exclusive use of Smedley's Hydro clientele. So this new church needed to be suitably imposing, even though financial restraints prevented the addition of a spire.

The Revd E. John Higgs gave land for the new church and vicarage, boosting the generosity of local philanthropists. Very tall mature trees now frame both buildings and All Saints' vicarage is one of a diminishing number still serving its original purpose. This early nineteenth-century postcard also shows Jackson House, then a hydro and now a hotel.

Matlock's past is written all over it and a wealth of detail, carved from Derbyshire stone, may go unnoticed above eye-level. Dale Road is especially rewarding. The group of women opposite the horse and carriage stand outside the old Town Hall/Market Hall. The watchmaker's premises in the foreground made way for a bank around 1913.

Forty or fifty years later, and parking was still possible on Dale Road, albeit on alternate sides. Today, an antiques centre occupies Marsden's department store, and the portico has gone from what was once a bank, afterwards solicitors' offices. The handsome Queen's Head Hotel (right foreground) has, in recent years, seen a variety of commercial ventures.

It might be difficult to identify this 1880s photograph without the unmistakable, turreted Olde English Hotel. Houses to the west of Dale Road are seen under construction, while shops on the opposite side have yet to be built. The grounds of the Olde English had tennis facilities and a cycle track used by Matlock Cycle Club.

Not quite a scene from the early days of cycling but Ron Duggins, out for a spin with his daughter, Corry, aged six. Twenty years on and Ron, a professional photographer, has progressed to a mountain bike and other racing machines. For the past two years, he has been a silver medal winner in the National Cyclo-Cross Championships.

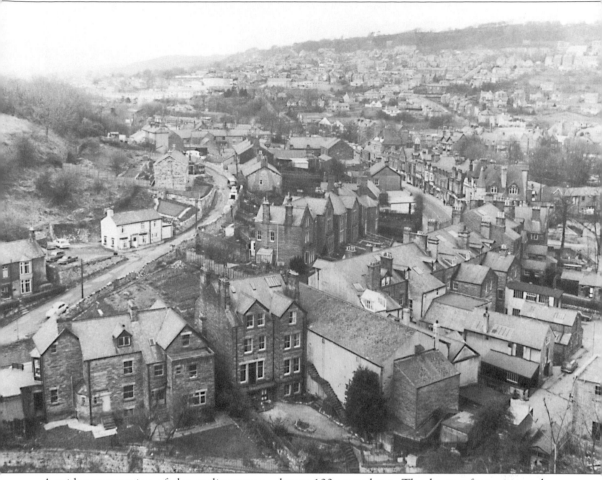

A wider perspective of the earlier scene, almost 100 years later. The houses first seen under scaffolding can be identified at centre, backing onto Holt Road, the original main thoroughfare between Matlock and Matlock Bath. The Olde English was supposedly rebuilt after a fire; properties in the foreground cover the open ground and cycle track of the earlier photograph.

Bank Road, originally Dob Lane, is the steep, direct route up Matlock Bank. This view slightly predates the new post office, built in 1912, at lower right. The first building beyond Lime Grove Walk is the police station, opposite the Town Hall. Large trees to the left of the road stand in Sparrow Park, formerly a public waste tip.

Eighty years later, and motorized traffic makes light work of Bank Road. Haydn Stanley's furniture store and a charity shop now come between the police station and the junction with Lime Grove Walk. Sparrow Park made way for the Lido buildings, until they were re-sited to make way for the Wilkinson store and a building society.

Firs Parade has not changed greatly since this early 1980s scene. The Woolworth's store and neighbouring shoe shop have been here since around 1954, and the Parade did not extend fully for several more years. New units opened in 1960, and one of the first occupants was Frank Clay; he later moved his decorating business across the road where it still trades under different ownership.

Pictured on active service in Kenya in 1943, Frank Clay was wounded during evacuation from Dunkirk, but subsequently took part in the Desert War and the Siege of Tobruk. He was still to be found behind the counter on Firs Parade, even in his late eighties. Frank Clay died in September 2000, aged 89.

In earlier times, the Duke of Wellington provided both accommodation and refreshment, but it was then very much on the outskirts of town – from here, the Chesterfield road headed towards open countryside. Since this photograph of 1893, the Duke has been extended, the road widened and the tollhouse on the right of the picture demolished.

Members of the Evans family stand outside the Horse Shoe Hotel, held by their ancestors and descendants for several generations. It was also a posting house, with stabling and coach houses and a blacksmith's and wheelwright shop in the rear yard. The pub was renowned for 'Old Tom', a potent brew rationed to two pints per customer in their own interests.

Five
Public Pride

The size of this smart turnout by Matlock fire brigade is consistent with the 1890s, when Capt. William Hodgson had a company of one lieutenant and ten men. The horse-drawn fire engine was garaged at the Town Hall from 1899, in which year a disastrous fire was fought in the centre of Matlock. The blaze broke out near Parr's Bank on Matlock Bridge, just before two o'clock on a Sunday morning in February and, by the time the bank manager raised the alarm, it had taken hold of the library and stationery business of Fred Else (now the NatWest bank) before spreading to Marsden's clothing store next door. Within half an hour, Capt. Hodgson of Matlock fire brigade had attached a hose to the nearest hydrant and the engine was being dragged down from the Town Hall by sheer manpower ,while other hands fetched and harnessed the horses. Telegrams were dispatched to neighbouring brigades at Bakewell, Lea Mills and Belper and it was 10 a.m. before the fight was won, helped by a heavy snowfall, which also dispersed the crowds.

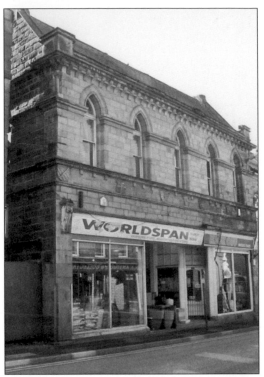

A row of carved stone shields gives a clue to the origins of this building on Dale Road. It opened in 1868 as Matlock's first Town Hall, with an assembly room, later used as a court room, banking rooms and offices. The ground floor Market Hall contained twelve glass-fronted shops along two sides, with two rows of open stalls down the centre.

After many years of earnest discussions by the Local Board, the former Bridge House Hydro for ministers and Christians was extended to become Matlock Town Hall in 1899. The kitchens were shared with the telephone exchange, newly relocated from the old Town Hall, while another part of the building became the headquarters of Derbyshire Yeomanry Cavalry.

Leather boots have given way to wellingtons, and jaunty berets to shiny brass helmets, for this fire brigade of the inter-war years. Only the uniform badges of their predecessors, and apparently the jackets, are unchanged. None of the moustached faces from the earlier photograph are recognizable; the men on the right are probably mechanics.

A presentation group outside New Street fire station in 1954. From left to right, back row: Mr Crowter, Maurice Hague, Harry Hague, Tom Fletcher, Frank Paxton, Harry Whitworth, Noel Birch. Front row: Reg Dixon, Phil Raynes, -?-, Bert Thomas, Robert Allsopp, Ernie Farnsworth, Les Sellers, Stan Stewart, Arthur Andrews, D.O. Richardson, Mr Swift.

Matlock police force of 1924 had expanded considerably from the unit of five constables and an inspector at the beginning of the century. The police station moved from Church Street to purpose-built premises on Bank Road in 1893. Seated third from the right is Inspector Kennedy, whose military bearing was much admired when he put his men through their weekly drill on New Street.

Six almshouses were endowed on Causeway Lane in 1898 by Miss Margaret Harrison, in memory of her brother, Dr William Harrison JP ... 'that the worthy poor, who may from time to time live in these dwellings, may enjoy peace and rest during the autumn of their lives.' There is always a waiting list for the cottages, should a vacancy arise.

Dress style excepted, this summery scene from the 1950s could be seen in Hall Leys Park today. In 1898, a large area of land from the river bank to Hall Leys Fields, and, in the other direction, from Crown Square to Knowleston Place, was given by Henry Knowles 'as a public promenade and pleasure resort for ever'.

Forty years later, and the park is under snow for this Christmas scene around the old tram shelter. A century earlier, the shelter had been officially opened in Crown Square in arctic conditions after heavy snowfalls. Nevertheless, a large crowd watched Mrs Wildgoose start the clock, before they all followed a brass band in a torchlit struggle up to Victoria Hall.

Silent films were shown at Victoria Hall until the Picture Palace – now an auctioneer's showroom – opened on Dale Road in 1913. The far grander Cinema House of 1922 had an orchestra and a deep stage for live shows, also a café and lounge. This 1950s postcard reveals that the cinema had yet to be renamed the Ritz.

The first shop after the cinema, undergoing alterations on the previous picture, became Farmer's electrical store in 1956. Charles Farmer had started out in the motor business with his brother Frank on Smedley Street and, in the 1930s, established a new sideline from a wooden shed beside the pumps, charging accumulators for and repairing wireless sets.

After a long struggle to stay open, the Ritz cinema has finally closed. It enjoyed its moment of glory quite late in life when, on 23 September 1996, it premièred Franco Zeffirelli's Jane Eyre. Starring William Hurt and Charlotte Gainsbourg, the film was shot on location at Haddon Hall. The Ritz rolled out the red carpet, but the leading stars had other commitments.

Matlock and District Operatic Society was founded in 1907. Members of this 1961 cast of *The White Horse Inn* performed on the stage of the Ritz cinema, are, from left to right, back row: Frank Clay, Harry Briddon, Fred Shaw, Derek Grattidge, Paul Dennison. Front row: Cyril Hunter, Brenda Gretton, Sheila Akers, Daphne Rice, Cora Oliver.

Not amateur dramatics exactly, but market trader, the late Bill Clay. He followed his father, 'Barrow Boy Ben', and grandfather into the business and here strikes a typically ebullient pose in front of his fruit and veg stall. Bill's trademark was his handlebar moustache, arguably the most luxuriant in town, but he was also the master of market-day banter.

In the mid-nineteenth century, the heart of old Matlock was Church Street, where the market cross stood 'by a fine lime tree', though the market itself had lapsed. Regular cattle markets and livestock fairs were later held at Matlock Green, but the general market was revived on a more central site adjoining the bus station, seen here in the 1970s.

Only twenty years ago, this was the scene behind the Lido, fronting onto Bakewell Road. The market stalls are huddled at the far side of the bus station, all of which disappeared under what was then known as the Fine Fare development, to be re-sited under cover beside the present Somerfield supermarket.

The Lido chimney and various buildings on the previous picture put this photograph into perspective. It is February 1983, and the first bricks are about to be laid on the town centre's £2 million supermarket development. While work was in progress, the market was transferred to the car park in front of the Town Hall.

From high above the development, the crane driver has the best view in Matlock, obviously sharing his cabin for the purposes of this bird's-eye view. Construction vehicles are working on the area of the new bus station, prior to work on the upper level car park. Imperial Road cuts diagonally across the picture.

Six

In the News

A poll on 20 June 1907 returned John Bertram Marsden-Smedley to a seat on the county council, filling a vacancy caused by the death of Job Smith. A wealthy, non-political candidate, Mr Marsden-Smedley took great delight in personally chauffeuring to the polls Matlock's oldest inhabitant, the bewhiskered Mr Thomas Green, ninety-five years old that very day. This faded but historic picture by Matlock photographer W.N. Statham shows the car, decorated with ribbons and flowers, as it passes under the railway bridge on Dale Road. Another point of interest is the proximity of quarrying activity so close to the road beyond the bridge, on an area which is now landscaped.

Royal visitors have been frequent guests of the Dukes of Devonshire, usually alighting at Rowsley station. On 12 December 1913, however, Queen Mary passed through Matlock on her way to Chatsworth, and this uniformed detachment of the Red Cross lined up in the town centre as her guard of honour.

This winning team of footballers mustered by a small out-of-town church are the Farley Congregationals, champions of West Derbyshire Amateur League and Fengl Cup winners, 1921/22. From left to right, back row: R. Hewitson, ? Semour, F. Fentem, A. Boden, E. Spencer, W. Osborne. Front row: ? Acton, D. Bagshaw, F. Wildgoose, ? Fentem, R. Else.

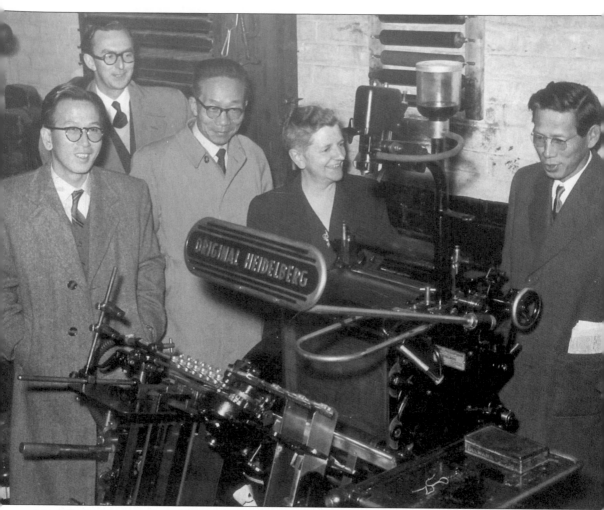

Mrs Ella Smith, founder of the *Matlock Mercury* and *West Derbyshire News*, showing a post-war group of Korean newspaper editors around Smith's printing works on Bakewell Road. Ella launched the Mercury in 1950, as a successor to her earlier publication, Coming Events, and remained closely associated with the newspaper for the rest of her life.

Herbert Duggins, a long-standing employee of Smith's printing works and Matlock Mercury, became a director shortly after this picture from around 1949/50. Here, he enjoys a brief respite from the pressures of typesetting. Herbert's sons have maintained a long family connection with the firm, Ron Duggins having taken numerous outstanding photographs for the Mercury over many years.

Her Majesty the Queen arrives at Matlock station in May 1992, at the start of an official royal visit. Here, she walks past a British Legion guard of honour, lined up beside the former station master's house, one of a number of railway buildings on the Ambergate/Rowsley line attributed to Joseph Paxton.

The outline of an archway at Harley House on Steep Turnpike suggests former use as a toll bar. In 1883, the house was the scene of a tragedy when the Revd Julius Benn was felled with a chamber pot by his troubled son, William. Julius was great-grandfather to former MP Tony Benn. William recovered his sanity to become the father of actress Margaret Rutherford, before suffering a further, permanent breakdown.

This excited crowd outside Farmer's looks like a queue for the sales, but had apparently gathered to watch a football match on television screens inside the store, possibly the 1966 World Cup. Charles Farmer ran a successful campaign to bring forward, by several years, better television viewing in the Derbyshire Dales, long a reception 'black spot'.

As the seat of Derbyshire county council, Matlock has attracted all sorts of demonstrations and protests. One of the liveliest was in November 1989, when over 500 union delegates gathered at County Hall to lobby against council spending cuts. Protesters 'seeped' through the building to gatecrash a meeting and police finally sealed off the room.

Typical of countrywide 'Ban the Bomb' demonstrations in the mid-1980s, these supporters of the Campaign for Nuclear Disarmament march through town, stopping traffic as they cross the bridge and head towards Dale Road. Bakewell and Matlock groups lead the way, followed by the New Mills contingent with a banner bearing the familiar CND symbol.

Seven
Jaunts and Journeys

The tram shelter was erected at the lower terminus in Crown Square in 1899, the gift of Robert Wildgoose. The stretch of road from here to Matlock Green was the occasional setting for scenes echoing Chariots of Fire, when young men competed to race the entire distance in the time it took for the clock to strike twelve. After the tramway ceased operations in 1927, the main section of the shelter, with its ever-useful clock tower, was relocated on Park Head. A smaller section served as a bus shelter next to Geoff Stevens' shop on Causeway Lane, but had to be dismantled after being set on fire. The inscribed stained-glass inserts have found a most appropriate home just a few miles away at Crich Tramway Village.

Joseph Allen & Sons provided the transport for this jaunt, a 1914 Farley Congregational Sunday school treat. Joseph himself is driving the first carriage, the Forget-Me-Not; the other three drivers are believed to be the '& Sons' of the family firm, founded around 1900. This type of transport was now steadily giving way to the motor bus.

This magnificent turn-out is lined up outside the Bakewell Road livery stables, built in 1899 for William Furniss. Backing up into Crown Square, the carriages are packed tight with excursionists, and there is not a bare head in sight. William took special pride in his smart, top-hatted coachmen and matching teams of horses.

This was the vehicle of choice in the post-war years, although its passengers look every bit as cramped as in days of yore. However, early buses could achieve ten miles per hour on the open road! R1693 was operated by Hand & Son, who also introduced half-hourly buses to Tansley; the fare was one penny to Matlock and threehalfpence back.

Travelling by carriage from Matlock to Derby was nothing out of the ordinary for William Smith, but this was 1944 and he was the front-seat passenger enjoying a family jaunt. Around 1914, William had driven the very last stagecoach from Sheffield to Baslow and, in the 1940s, founded the Darley School of Equitation, forerunner of Red House Stables, which remains with the family.

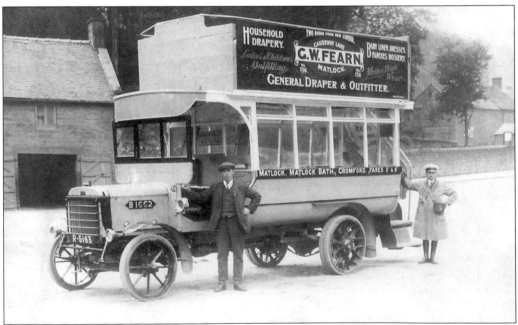

This double-decker bus was built by the London General Omnibus Company, a 'B type', which they started selling off in 1920. The Derbyshire registration number dates to the same year, and it is believed that only Hands were running double-deckers at this time. The 'new cinema' referred to on the advertisement board was built in 1922.

By the 1920s, Joseph Allen & Son had taken over Furniss's Crown Square premises and this motorized hearse and mourning cars were available for hire. The open space to the left is now a supermarket, while the Victorian buildings are newly transformed into The Crown, the third licensed premises in the vicinity to trade under this name.

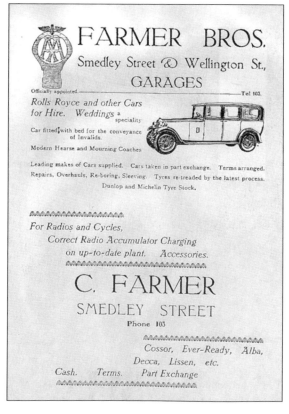

Farmers' Garage is a rare survivor from the hydro era. From its beginnings in car hire over eighty years ago, the family firm now specializes in 4 x 4 vehicles. There are still a few local folk who can recall pulling up at Farmers' pumps for National Benzole or Cleveland at barely a shilling a gallon.

Matlock tramway opened in March 1893. Guest of honour was Job Smith, manager of the tramway company, here facing outwards from the centre of the upper deck. The public-spirited Smith had worked for years to introduce a tramway to his home town, and he personally gained financial backing from the publisher George (later Sir George) Newnes.

The cable system kept two counterbalanced trams in synchronized use, one running uphill and one down. This wide expanse at the Bank Road/Smedley Street crossroads provided a passing loop, virtually outside the doors of Smedley's Hydro. When off duty, the trams were garaged alongside a standby vehicle at the Rutland Street depot.

Seen here in 1988, the tram depot originally had an engine room/repair shop and a boiler house with two massive steam boilers powering the underground tramway cable. The upper terminus offered a waiting room and 'passenger convenience'. The buildings have had several different uses, and the old boilerhouse chimney is reduced to a shadow of its former self.

The trams went, and the one-penny downhill rides with them, so in the 1930s, there was nothing for it but to step out – these three smart young things have Bank Road to themselves and the mighty Masson Hill provides a stunning backdrop to their descent. Motor cars and buses continued to avoid the route for many more years.

Steep Turnpike is another road banned to heavy vehicles. The name aptly identifies this 1:7 hill as the start of the old turnpike road to Chesterfield. A favourite descent for sledging in days long past, it still presents problems as soon as snow starts to fall. Behind the hedge and tall trees is The Firs, home to Matlock Library.

The reason for its delightful name escapes us, but there is no denying the blip in The Dimple. The old route eastwards into Matlock used to curve around Hackney Lane to drop steeply down The Dimple, which has, at various times, been home to farmers, butchers, hosiery manufacturers, a bootmaker, a joiner, a blacksmith, a tripe dresser and a factory producing salt twists for crisps.

The Matlocks have never lost their popularity, but in 1968, the scenic line between Matlock and Buxton was felled by the Beeching Axe. This evocative photograph of 1957, taken from High Tor, shows a 4F loco and eight-carriage excursion train puffing its way through Matlock Dale on the way home to south Derbyshire.

This British Rail excursion bill dates from eight years later, when ramblers still had a line to take them into the heart of prime walking country. They could journey across the spectacular Miller's Dale viaduct and gain access to the beautiful limestone hills and dales of the White Peak, with further connections at Buxton.

In 1975, a group of enthusiasts formed the Peak Railway Society with the aim of re-opening the line between Matlock and Buxton, so restoring a direct Derby-Manchester link. This volunteer body gave rise to Peak Rail plc which has so far reinstated the line between Matlock and Rowsley South. Here, we see track-laying at Matlock in 1979.

These overgrown tracks of 1982 would have been unthinkable in times past. A hundred years earlier, quarry owners and stone merchants had extensive yards and wharves in the station yard. Scores of masons were at work dressing stone, much of it destined for overseas. T.C. Drabble exported stone to Australia; Matlock millstones ground wood pulp for the paper industries of Norway, the USA and the Colonies; and Poor Lots Quarry at Tansley provided particularly fine grindstones for the manufacture of needles, glass stoppers, cutlery and files. Several coal merchants also had wharves at the station, meeting the never-ending need for coal from gas works and the hydros.

Darley Dale is the intermediate station on the re-opened line, pictured in 1996, with Peak Rail volunteers laying the first track ready to head towards Matlock. In 2000, the project moved a step closer when the Government announced an improvement package for Britain's public transport network and acknowledged the importance of re-opening the Matlock-Buxton line.

1996 again, and volunteers enjoy an evening special, laid on as a shared treat at the end of another tiring day. During the following year, the northern extension to the former Rowsley locomotive depot saw its first passenger trains for almost thirty years. Peak Rail now operates steam trains all year round.

Eight
At Work and Play

Harvest time at one of the once-numerous small farms on the outskirts of Matlock. The tradition of providing the labourers with ample quantities of harvest ale prevailed throughout the Peak, though here the whole family has turned out to help – and probably the neighbours too, who would be repaid with free labour in return. Every year, scores of men could be seen spreading across the moors around Rushley Farm, cutting heather to be taken to Matlock station and sent away for making besoms. At one time, all the farms on Matlock Moor, from Amber Hill to Packhorse, Sycamore and Portland Grange, took their milk to Matlock. Their horse-drawn floats went from house to house, selling un-bottled milk from measures, straight to the jug.

Matlock Town Football Club dates back to at least the 1890s and played on the Hall Leys before Causeway Lane. This junior team of 1916 includes Herbert Smith, standing next to the soldier in the back row. As proprietor of Smith's printing works, Herbert became publisher of the Matlock Mercury.

With Miss Addy at centre front, these ladies formed the refreshment committee for a police and tradesmen charity cricket match on 3 July 1930. Matlock Cricket Club has played on this Causeway Lane meadow for ninety years, having moved from adjoining land when the football club moved there.

The town has a long musical tradition of a high order, and several names still command respect, not least Lubin Wildgoose. With his double bass, he cuts an imposing figure as the central member of Matlock Brotherhood Orchestra, seated around Hall Leys bandstand in the 1920s.

This rather earlier photograph shows that outlying villages could also put on a good show. Darley Wakes were led by this Rum-Tum Band – the usually more sedate Darley Band in holiday disguise. The donkey never took to the streets without a bottle of 'oil' for the bath chair, but it was an open secret that the bottle contained something to oil the bandsmen.

Matlock Carnival always enjoys great local support, with decorated floats and a procession through town. This wonderful beast took part in the 1937 carnival and is an example of the genus 'sprog'. Pram wheels are just visible beneath the massive papier maché head, but the seven or eight men inside the canvas body are completely hidden.

The attractions of Hall Leys Park have all stood the test of time, especially the miniature railway. Here, the train sets out along the line on 19 August 1961, owned at that time by Mr Swain. The loco, known as 2701, was built around 1949 by Stanley Battison of Ilkeston, and was painted in chocolate-red livery.

This ambitious 'leisure centre' was built on Smedley Street in 1895. Dances, boxing and fencing matches were laid on in the 700-seat concert hall, and sports facilities included tennis courts, bowling green, swimming pool and roller-skating rink. Victoria Hall never truly lived up to expectations and lasted barely twenty years. It was finally demolished in the 1990s.

Victoria Hall was used in the First World War as a factory making woollen clothing for soldiers. It subsequently passed to the Derwent Mills Company, producers of Furida knitting wool, who, in the late 1920s, ran a nationwide competition which overwhelmed Matlock post office with thousands of packages sent in response. Paton & Baldwin's took over production in 1931, some ten years before the date of this photograph.

Paton & Baldwin's provided a good number of jobs for women, many walking to work from outlying villages. One lady, now in her eighties, who then lived on Riber hill, tells of walking the three miles to work and back, with a long tiring climb in each direction ... and putting in a half-day on Saturdays. This picture was taken around 1950.

Men at Wildgoose's gritstone quarry on Matlock Moor down tools for Matlock photographer William Statham. Some quarrymen's families lived on nearby Quarry Lane, in houses built and owned by Wildgoose's. A resident of the 1930s recalls the properties as then being very damp and tells how the menfolk disliked living so close to their work.

This low-tech machinery represented the first attempt at mechanization in Cawdor quarry around 1946, with Fred Gill standing left of Alf Bunting. Quarrying remains a major local industry, but the extensive Cawdor site is now derelict, awaiting promised major development in the form of housing and offices, a leisure centre and supermarket.

No hard hats for these rockmen inside Cawdor Quarry around 1937. Cawdor had its own sidings for transporting stone to the station. Much of the output from this, and other limestone quarries, fed the relentless demand for road stone and as a flux for blast furnaces, but many lives were severely shortened by 'mason's complaint', i.e. silicosis.

A vertiginous shot of workmen netting the face of Harvey Dale Quarry, during work on Tarmac's new offices in 1976. Previously owned by Derbyshire Stone Limited, Harvey Dale was historically the parish quarry. Although not by any means the largest of quarries, this picture gives some idea of why their existence excludes Matlock from the Peak District National Park.

When, in 1989, a giant waste disposal company planned to dump toxic waste in the disused Lumshill Quarry, within 200 yards of Highfields School, a thousand people took to the streets and marched on the County Offices. Organized by MAD – Matlock Against Dumping – the protest ensured that no toxic tipping took place.

Nine

The Old Town, Riber and Matlock Moor

Old Church, Matlock.

A century and a half ago, this was the centre of the old town around the parish church and green, the subject of this engraving of 1869. Although the stocks which stood in front of the Wheatsheaf Inn, in the background, are not in evidence, an elderly resident of the 1930s recalled finding a friend fastened in the stocks, protesting that he was being punished merely for 'wife clouting'. The great lime tree now has an equally mighty successor, planted in 1924, with, at its foot, the stump and socket of the probable market cross. Church Street drops into Matlock Green, with shops which, in their time, have provided everything from saddlery and harness to drapery and greengrocery. Within living memory, markets and fairs were held along the main road, with amusements set up on a field where the filling station now stands. At the May cattle fair – which was also a hiring fair – beasts and horses were sometimes lined up all the way from Steep Turnpike to Matlock Cliff.

Dedicated to St Giles, patron saint of beggars, cripples and blacksmiths, Matlock parish church stands in the earliest part of town. Very little of the Norman church survives; this photograph of 1862 shows the fifteenth-century edifice, prior to extensive alterations. One of the nine bells is of pre-Reformation date and is dedicated to St Mary Magdalene.

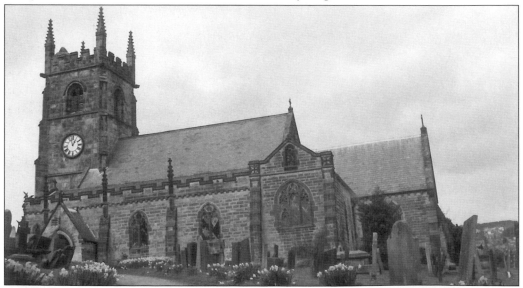

St Giles, at the dawn of a new millennium. Inside the church is a memorial to Adam and Grace Woolley, who shared a remarkable seventy-six years of married life. Adam died in 1657, aged almost 100, and Grace lived to almost 110. A very different tale lies behind the headstone of Sarah Smith: 'Short was her time in single life, Six times, seven years she was a wife ...'.

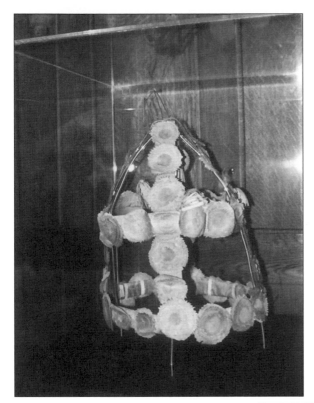

Six rare maidens' garlands, otherwise known as crants or crantsies, survive at St Giles'. These tributes to chastity and purity were carried at the funerals of young unmarried women, more than two centuries ago. This garland, typically a hooped wickerwork frame decorated with paper rosettes, flowers and ribbons, has recently been conserved and the others are in protective storage.

Stoney Way is part of a network of alleyways and paths descending from the church into Knowleston Place, where Victorian and Edwardian houses stand alongside old cottages with date-stones from 1621. Bentley Brook separates the dwellings from a massive limestone tor. At its foot, a small Victorian park with hollies, yews, fir trees and tufa rockeries.

This painting of unknown date shows part of the King's Head, most likely at the time when its landlord, like many country publicans, combined his living with farming. The old inn served the town for more than two centuries, but today an iron bracket is all that remains of its regal inn sign, though the stone mounting steps are still in place.

Here, the King's Head is open for business and decorated with a crown and various items, including what appear to be glass candle-jars. The occasion may be the Coronation of 1911. The banner across Church Street makes it clear that the assembly is proud to belong to the old part of Matlock town.

This handsome mansion behind the green on Church Street was once yet another hostelry of old Matlock, the Wheatsheaf Inn. Parts of the building are earlier than the date-stone inscribed 'WCS 1681'. In fairly recent times, the property was used as a pottery but, as seen on this modern picture, has now reverted entirely to residential occupation.

This pub is the last survivor of several which plied for business on Church Street. Duke William was William Augustus, Duke of Cumberland, and second son of George II. The Duke was almost at the height of his army career when this inn was built in 1734. By the following year, he was known as 'Butcher' Cumberland and out of public favour.

The gaunt Riber Castle occupies a magnificent position, 850ft above sea level. Built as a residence for John Smedley, it is seen here as a school between the wars. In the Second World War, the property became a storage depot and afterwards, as a semi-derelict ruin in 1963, a wildlife park. Now under new ownership, Riber Castle is currently at the centre of controversial development plans.

It was after the death of widowed Mrs Caroline Smedley, that Riber Castle became a boys' preparatory school. This group of 1923 has the younger gentlemen comfortably seated on a rug. At the centre of the second row are resident master, the Revd J.W. Chippett, with Mrs and Captain Lionel Gathorne Wilson, the principal.

Riber House Farm, on the hillside below the castle, was home for half a century to the related Farnsworth and Taylor families. This wedding group outside the farm around 1908 brings together, from left to right: Bill Farnsworth (the best man), bride Rose Farnsworth, Maggie and Olive Knowles (her nieces), groom William Todd, and chief bridesmaid May Farnsworth.

No less than sixteen related musicians and singers made up the Farnsworths' family choir; grandmas and granddads from two generations, uncles, aunts and cousins. At Christmas, they all dressed up, painted their faces and went 'guisering' (known elsewhere as 'mumming'), performing in houses and pubs of surrounding villages to collect for the Whitworth Hospital.

CHRISTMAS 1899.

Mr. FARNSWORTH wishes to thank the inhabitants of Matlock and District for past favours, and begs to announce that the well-known

Farnsworth's Family Choir

will again call at the principal places in Matlock and surrounding Districts during Christmas Week, singing Christmas Carols and Anthems, &c., as follows

Christians Awake!	Sing Sweet Carols
Hark the Herald Angels sing.	Blessing.
While Shepherds Watched	Lead, Kindly Light.
O. Come all ye Faithful.	Diadem.
Silent Night.	Cry Out and Shout.
Glad Tidings.	Hail! Smiling Morn.
Angels from the Realms of Glory.	Praise God from whom all Blessings flow.

VOCALISTS:

MRS. LUCY FARNSWORTH *GRANNIE*		MR. JNO. H. FARNSWORTH	
MISS ROSE *AUNTIE* „	TREBLE.	„ ALFRED *UNCLE* „	
MARY *GRANDMA*		„ TOM *UNCLE.* „	
MASTER BERTIE *UNCLE* HERBT. *UNCLE*		*GRANDAD*	
MRS. SARAH FARNSWORTH *AUNTIE*	ALTO.	MR. JOHN FARNSWORTH	
MISS VIOLET *AUNT* „		„ GEO. W. *GRANDAD.*	
MASTER PERCY *COUSIN* „		„ WALTER *UNCLE*	
		„ WILLIE *UNCLE*	
VIOLINIST - MR. WILFRED FARNSWORTH *UNCLE*			

Proceeds to be devoted to Charitable Purposes.

89

Scenes such as this at Starkholmes were not especially unusual around Matlock before the last war. Even Riber Castle relied on one good well for its water supply and this was shared with Riber House Farm, necessitating a daily uphill trek to fetch two pails of water on just such a yoke as this.

Hydropathy brought patients of all creeds and colours to Matlock, leading to a flurry of church-building to suit many types of worship. Of the four Primitive Methodist churches on this early twentieth-century postcard, only that on Matlock Moor is still used for worship, with regular and well-attended Sunday services.

Colonel H. Brooke-Taylor performs the first drive at the opening of Matlock Golf Course on 21 September 1907. The course was designed by professional golfer Tom Williamson and the Derbyshire Times agreed that it was 'an absolute necessity for any self-respecting health and holiday resort'. Proprietors and managers of the hydros had certainly been prime movers behind the venture.

Practically within striking distance of the golf course are these bee boles, or bee garths, almost hidden from view at the base of a drystone wall near Cuckoostone Quarry. Such deep recesses were built just above ground level to contain skeps – beehives made from straw – in order to protect them from the weather.

Edith Emeline Statham, née Young, with her first grandchild, George Statham, at Brickyard Farm in 1932. George is now in the family farm, built by the Youngs around 1850 using stone and bricks from their own quarry and brickyard. The Young/Statham families are descended from the Saxtons, who had shares in the Old Bath at Matlock Bath.

This young throng on John Else's field is celebrating the 1911 Coronation of King George V and Queen Mary. On what was obviously a bright, sunny day everyone is dressed in their Sunday best – one young fellow sports a straw boater, while the girls' bonnets would have graced a garden party.

The Wishing Stone is a massive rock above Lumsdale, one of the natural attractions sought by Victorian visitors as an escape from what a contemporary critic called 'the incursions of the *profanum vulgus*'. It was especially popular with romantic souls who came to walk around it three times, in the hope of being granted a wish.

A well-used path still brings walkers up to the Wishing Stone, if only to admire the view nowadays. The pretty Victorian shelter from the early twentieth-century picture above now stands beside the A632 Chesterfield road, offering seating and a breather for cyclists and walkers taking this long climb out of Matlock.

The steep woodland setting above Artists' Corner is captured in one of the many fine paintings by the late Frank Clay. A former pupil of Matlock Bath school, the artist also designed and painted set pieces for the Venetian Fêtes and Illuminations, choosing themes such as the Willow Pattern story, Alice in Wonderland and Snow White.

Matlock Bath

Ten

Underground, Overground

Almost 400ft high, this spectacular limestone outcrop looms over the Derwent between Matlock and Matlock Bath. High Tor caused wonderment to early travellers, and Victorian writers and artists took it to their hearts. This engraving is dated 1855. In *Gem of the Peak* (1843), William Adam enthuses over its 'towering majesty ... kissing the very heavens to mingle with the stars'. And moving on almost a century for a lady's viewpoint: ' ... in places there are glimpses of haunting beauty. On the left rises the glorious mass of High Tor ... with birches, oaks and mountain ash covering the lower slopes and grim, gaunt limestone above.' (Ethel Carleton Williams, *Companion into Derbyshire*)

The name of this lovely stretch of Matlock Dale speaks for itself. Here, a possibly late nineteenth-century aspect shows the toll gate, while countless painters and photographers have captured the wider scene, with its picturesque whitewashed cottages curving round the bend, the river Derwent and High Tor opposite.

The exposed perpendicular slopes of High Tor are an irresistible challenge to climbers, their bright helmets dotting the massive rock face all year round. The bare head of this fearless sportsman sets him a generation apart from today's better-equipped rock climbers. The section of road far below him is Dale Road, the A6.

The gabled houses on the preceding photograph were abandoned after a landslide left this scene of devastation. Major landslides in the dale are rare, but one nineteenth-century writer told of a wet season when the whole mass of a 'craggy perpendicular cliff' slid downhill onto the road, narrowly missing a passing chaise, full of travellers.

Adam's assurance that the stoutest heart would tremble on peering over the edge of the precipice was no exaggeration, and High Tor has solicited numerous accidents. Tragically, the casualty in this rescue attempt of 1936 died from his injuries. His name was Eddie Watkins, a Welshman who fell in love with the Dales while working at Lilybank Hydro.

High Tor is one of seven public pleasure grounds in the ongoing Matlock Parks Project, so improvements are in hand. Access to the grounds is free nowadays, but visitors once had to pay to ramble on High Tor and explore the Roman and Fern Caves – damp, deep fissures left from the outcropping of lead veins.

200 years ago, descendants of Sir Richard Arkwright improved the lead miners' paths over High Tor and planted large expanses of trees. 'Arkwright's Grand Tour' was then created to give a gradual ascent from Matlock. Refreshments were available at the summit – a facility sought in vain, since this wooden building burned down five years ago.

Facing High Tor is Masson Hill, with its major tourist attraction, the Heights of Abraham. This modern railway poster features the cable-car system, installed in the early 1980s, a transport well suited to the alpine scenery. On a busy day, the gondolas gently sweep as many as 4,000 passengers up and over the scenic gorge.

Formerly the Nestus lead mine, Great Rutland Cavern on the Heights of Abraham was renamed in honour of the Duke of Rutland, on opening as a show cavern in 1810. Early tourists to the Nestus system had no access other than the mine shafts, and had only candles for illumination. This postcard shows owner Samuel Sprinthall at centre in the early 1900s.

100

'We went in this cavern this morning' writes the sender of this 1914 postcard, but unfortunately she does not elaborate. However, the Peak District Mines Historical Society connects the cavern's name with the Hopping and Jacob's lead mines beneath Upperwood; their extensive fluorspar workings were once partly open as show-places.

Research by members of the same society confirms this location as Hopping Mine, around 1920. The high grade fluorspar mine was operated by George Crowther, here standing in the doorway of his office. Henry Botham stands in front of him and the group to the right includes Henry's brother, Albert, and Sam Webster.

The Peak District Mining
Museum has gone a long way to
giving the Grand Pavilion a new
lease of life, in fact, the newly
painted building is literally in
the pink. Lead mining is the
region's oldest industry, and the
museum is a lively repository for
rusty relics, yellowed documents,
ancient wagons and massive
machinery retrieved from
abandoned mines.

Nick Hardie, here a student and
now an Inspector of Mines,
photographed by Richard Bird in
early 1983, during work to re-
open Temple Mine as part of the
Mining Museum. Visitors can
now pan for minerals at this
former fluorspar and lead mine –
samples have been found to
contain gold at a respectable 37
grammes per ton.

The thermal waters which emerge in Matlock Bath gave the village both its name and fame. For almost a century, the Whittaker family utilized this natural resource in bottled mineral waters and soft drinks. Matlock Bath Aërated and Mineral Water works stood in the Dale, but were demolished after production ended around thirty years ago.

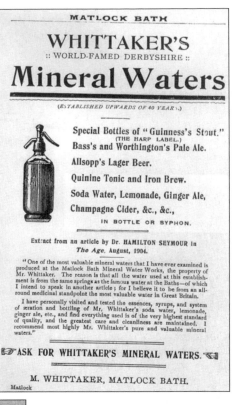

Labels and bottles survive as souvenirs of the late-lamented 'pop factory'. Stories lie behind two of the labels: 'Kitty Kola' was Whittaker's response to legal threats from a certain American giant, while hundreds of unused 'High Tor' labels had to be scrapped when it transpired that an Australian brand already used the same name.

Various petrifying wells formerly displayed objects being 'turned to stone'. Everything imaginable was arranged under a constant spray of the heavily mineralized waters, to be transformed under a gradual build-up of lime: baskets of fruit, ferns, human and other skulls, wigs, lanterns, shoes, toys, and birds' nests, complete with eggs. Only one well maintains the tradition today.

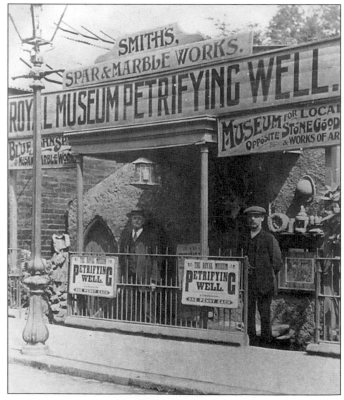

This petrifying well adopted its name after a visit in 1832 by the young Princess Victoria, who also toured the spar shops and museums. Matlock Bath gave her a truly royal welcome; fir trees had been felled from the Heights of Abraham and re-erected, festooned with flowers and garlands, alongside the royal route.

This late nineteenth/early twentieth-century stereoscopic card shows the thermal fishpond with a slot machine on the railings. A penny bought a small cardboard-boxful of fish food, such as dried grubs and shrimps. The council paid 6d for wasps' nests; these and their grubs were broken up and packaged for the machines.

In the right-hand wall of the fishpond, as seen from the front, is a barely legible underwater milestone dated 1801. It originally stood outside the livery stables, which made way for the Pavilion, but was re-sited beside the then clay-bottomed pond. When the pond was remodelled, the water level rose above the milestone.

Water power was used to operate a switchback in the Derwent Gardens. With or without the doctor's advice to take half-a-dozen rides for the benefit of one's liver, the switchback carried thousands of passengers on a good Bank Holiday, and it was known for proprietor Mr Buxton to take home his takings in a wheelbarrow!

The switchback was dismantled in 1934. Few illustrations exist, but it does appear in the background of this delightful postcard of 1905, showing a trio of girls with their hoops on Lovers' Walks. The word 'Switchback' appears on the building over the river, with the supports and track visible to the right.

Eleven

Life in a Resort

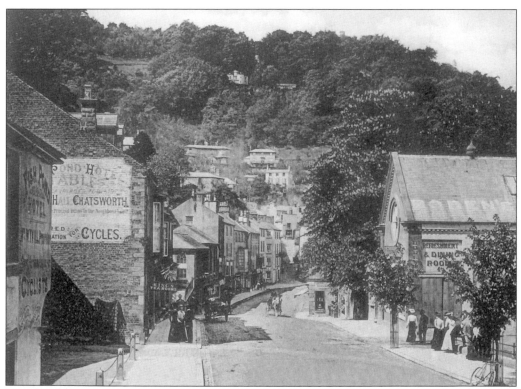

This late Victorian view of South Parade looks from the Fish Pond Hotel towards the bend which was to become such a bottleneck for motor traffic. The four-storey building jutting onto the path by the bend was, and still is, Hodgkinson's Hotel, offering good stabling and a change of horses for coach travellers. Originally part of the Great Hotel, Hodgkinson's also boasted one of the best cellars in the kingdom, thanks to a year-round coolness from being built against the rock. Boden's Restaurant, in the right foreground, catered for large community events, as well as tourists, but was demolished many years ago. New shop units have recently been built on the site.

In 1849, the railway opened up Matlock Bath to the hoi polloi, and the epithet 'Little Switzerland', born of a compliment from Lord Byron, inexorably gave way to 'Little Blackpool'. Compared with this photograph of 1888/89, there is now just a single line which ends at the next station, Matlock – the 'up' platform, signal box and footbridge are all gone.

This railway poster promotes a regular annual event held at the Grand Pavilion. For those who preferred the outdoors, there were weekend excursion tickets, though one guidebook dutifully warned ladies who objected to climbing walls, that stiles in the Peak were often remarkably narrow – 6in being considered a liberal allowance.

The two hotels nearest the station, seen here around 1890, are still in business. To the left is The Midland and, at far right, the County and Station, bordering Holme Road. The old police station was just around this corner, a small house where the sergeant could offer overnight accommodation in a cramped cell with iron bars.

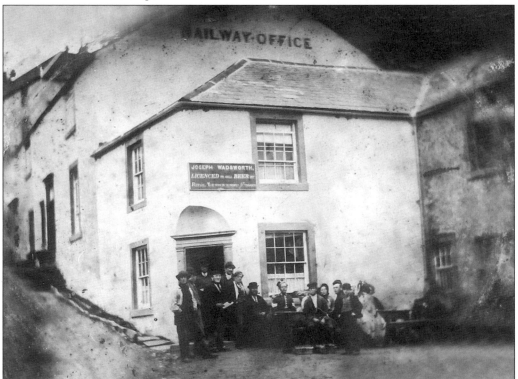

Since there are ladies present, the main business of this group outside the Fish Pond Hotel around 1895 is probably to do with its role as railway booking office. In earlier times, under the ownership of the Old Bath establishment, this hotel was known as the Old Bath Tap.

The main thoroughfare through Matlock Bath follows North and South Parades. North Parade has lost far fewer buildings to road widening, development having been confined to the side away from the river. The continuous chain of shops and restaurants remain much as they appear on this early twentieth-century postcard.

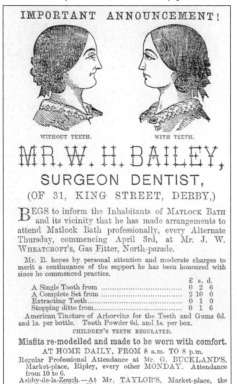

IMPORTANT ANNOUNCEMENT!

WITHOUT TEETH.   WITH TEETH.

MR. W. H. BAILEY,
SURGEON DENTIST,
(OF 31, KING STREET, DERBY,)

BEGS to inform the Inhabitants of MATLOCK BATH and its vicinity that he has made arrangements to attend Matlock Bath professionally, every Alternate Thursday, commencing April 3rd, at Mr. J. W. WHEATCROFT's, Gas Fitter, North-parade.

Mr. B. hopes by personal attention and moderate charges to merit a continuance of the support he has been honoured with since he commenced practice.

	£	s.	d.
A Single Tooth from	0	2	6
A Complete Set from	2	10	0
Extracting Teeth	0	1	0
Stopping ditto from	0	1	6

American Tincture of Arborvitæ for the Teeth and Gums 6d. and 1s. per bottle. Tooth Powder 6d. and 1s. per box.

CHILDREN'S TEETH REGULATED.

Misfits re-modelled and made to be worn with comfort.

AT HOME DAILY, FROM 8 a.m. TO 8 p.m.

Regular Professional Attendance at Mr. G. BUCKLAND'S, Market-place, Ripley, every other MONDAY. Attendance from 10 to 6.

Ashby-de-la-Zouch.—At Mr. TAYLOR'S, Market-place, the Third SATURDAY in each Month. Attendance from 12 to 6.

According to this 'Important Announcement' from The Matlock Companion of 1862, North Parade was just the place for an ambitious surgeon dentist to set up a fortnightly practice. The expression 'Misfits re-modelled' must be assumed to relate to false teeth, and not to his patients!

The Victoria Jubilee Promenade and the ornamental iron footbridge over the Derwent were constructed to mark Queen Victoria's Golden Jubilee in 1887. This rare postcard, of around 1905, shows the Promenade with the kiosk and turnstile which gave admission to the footbridge, so linking the Promenade with Lovers' Walks across the river.

Lovers' Walks were also accessible by ferry, a manually-operated wire cable hauling the boat from bank to bank. This ferry near the Pavilion is pictured around 1912. During the First World War, a Canadian soldier, stationed at the Royal Hotel, accepted a bet to pull himself across the wire, hand over hand. Sadly, he lost his grip, fell in and his body was never recovered.

The same ferry from the opposite riverbank, overlooked by three important buildings: Holy Trinity church, the Royal Hotel and, just visible at top right, the old Pavilion of 1884. Also known as the Palais Royal, this ambitious structure had a 228ft, mainly glass, frontage and occupied a magnificent position on the Heights of Jacob.

The new Pavilion of 1910 is central to this postcard dated the following year. The spar shop in the foreground is long gone, but the 'rude grit stone obelisk', mentioned by William Adam in 1843, still guards the road to the Temple Hotel. In Adam's day, the road also climbed to the Old Bath.

Pictured shortly before it burned down in 1928, the Royal Hotel was built fifty years earlier to replace the historic Old Bath. The new establishment boasted extensive and immaculately maintained grounds and, like its predecessor, took full advantage of the thermal waters. Russian, Turkish, vapour and a variety of other treatment baths were on offer.

The skeleton of the Royal Hotel was demolished after the fire. The site is now Temple Road car park, where the spring which fed the Old Bath still flows beneath a tufa grotto engraved 'Royal Well founded 1696'. The waters disappear and re-emerge on their descent to the Derwent Gardens, before finally mingling with the river.

This wonderful crowded scene on South Parade was captured on another stereoscopic photograph by Alfred Seaman, at some time between the 1880s and 1910. Matlock Bath has been a favourite subject since the days of the earliest photographers, and a number of studios were established here, including that of Seaman, to whom I have already referred.

The buildings are easily matched to the above picture, but how very different is the twenty-first-century scene. Matlock Bath has become a weekend Mecca for hundreds of bikers – many of them 'born again' – here to mingle happily with less focused visitors as they wander up and down, casting a critical eye along the competition.

The central figure here is the late Remo Tinti, 'The Man in the White Suit', for many years Compère of the Illuminations and all-round ambassador for the Matlocks. Pictured with Councillor Tinti are, from left to right: Mr and Mrs John Broome and Sir George and Lady Kenning. Sir George had just opened the 1954 Venetian Fête.

From August to the end of October, the Illuminations add a touch of magic to the village's lovely setting, with miles of coloured bulbs reflected in the Derwent. Weekends bring 'The Venetian Nights', with fireworks and a parade of decorated and illuminated boats on the river, their boatmen blending imperceptibly into the darkness.

Matlock Bath Illuminations began with celebrations for Queen Victoria's Diamond Jubilee in 1897. Candles and coloured flares supplied lights in the early years, and some of the Victorian candle-glasses are still in use, seen here being lit and suspended around a Chinese pagoda before its launch on the river in September 2000.

A very different season beautifies the fountain beside Clifton Road in January 1982. Derbyshire was icebound, leaving the authorities overwhelmed by calls from tenants with frozen and burst pipes. The thermal fountains went beyond the usual winter spectacle of producing clouds of steam and finally succumbed to the deep freeze.

Twelve
Village Life

This souvenir of a works outing from the Via Gellia Colour Company dates from around 1912. The workers would all have been local men, but ventured no further than the old Pavilion for their day out, posing for a photograph in the grounds. At the centre of the front row is works foreman Mr Teasdale, holding a half-empty box of cigars. He has obviously distributed his largesse, since most of the men are holding, if not smoking, a cigar – the lad at top right looks particularly pleased with himself.

The riverside road through Matlock Bath formerly connected with the Nottingham to Newhaven turnpike at Cromford. Two toll gates existed in the vicinity of Masson Mills; this one is Warm Wells toll cottage, with picture postcards displayed in a side window. Simons & Pickard's paper mill is just in sight further down the road.

Masson chimney serves to place buildings formerly located at the cobbled foot of The Wapping, an ancient way to Upperwood. Long before this 1960s photograph, the bay-windowed house was Hot Springs Toll House, its taller neighbour, the Red Lion Inn. Both are gone now, but the pub cellars can still be seen as caves below the road to the New Bath Hotel.

The old Pavilion, or Palais Royal, opened in 1884. For many years, it had a resident orchestra and the main stage was graced by the likes of Sarah Bernhardt and Mrs Patrick Campbell, while band contests drew guardsmen, highlanders in full dress and cavalry bands with kettle drums. The site is now part of Gulliver's Kingdom.

The Pavilion was a great seasonal asset, but also very much the villagers' leisure centre. Here they could attend dog and cat shows, poultry exhibitions, flower shows, puppet theatres, Christmas pantomimes and the cream of minstrel shows. This gilded ticket gave admittance to the Coronation festivities of Edward VII and Queen Alexandra.

The new Pavilion was built by a German contractor in 1910, and was first known as the Kursaal, the German word for a spa establishment. The timing of the name, and the expense, was unfortunate, being followed so soon by the outbreak of war, and, not surprisingly, the edifice became better known as the Grand Pavilion.

For some years from the 1940s, Matlock and District Chamber of Trade held biennial exhibitions in the Pavilion. Well-known personalities opened the proceedings, in this instance, BBC Television presenter and housewives' 'heart-throb', McDonald Hobley. Hands behind his back, 'Mac' poses with Charles Farmer, proprietor of the radio and television stand.

This was Perry's glove factory, the day after it burned out in 1929. It stood behind Boden's Restaurant, and the owner continued in business by setting up frames inside the nearby Pavilion, using machinery powered by a massive gas engine. Taylors of Cromford also used the ground floor for silk throwing.

During the First World War, almost forty auxiliary hospitals were established in Derbyshire for the care of wounded servicemen. Many hydros and large hotels were taken over for this purpose and the Royal Hotel became a hospital for Canadian officers. Maple leaf cap badges identify this group on the road up to the hospital.

One of the last major events at the Royal Hotel was this visit in 1928 by Lord Baden-Powell, here to inspect Scout troops while attending a conference at Smedley's Hydro. The plain wooden structure at centre left bears the sign 'Artistic Photography', though the far end of the building was used by Slater the tailor.

With their jaunty straw boaters and starched shirts, these 1920s bandsmen take a breather from entertaining the crowds in Derwent Gardens. Outdoor entertainment is still a regular attraction here and a great deal of musical activity takes place around the bandstand all summer long.

The banks of the Derwent have long been the setting for many other festivities than the luminescent Venetian Nights. This summertime poster promised a festive day, with some events on the river itself, all brought to a spectacular conclusion with a 'Sylvan Illumination' and more besides.

MATLOCK BATH
FLORAL
AND
RIVER FÊTE
Saturday, July 16th, 1938.

FLORAL DECORATED PROMENADES.

POTTED SPORTS :——
CRICKET,
HORSE RACES,
BURLESQUE.
FASHION PARADES, MYSTERY ITEMS,
Played and Featured on the River Derwent.

DANCES ✳ BANDS ✳ ETC.

GIGANTIC ATTRACTIONS!
Commencing 3 p.m.   8 hours Continuous Amusement.

MAMMOTH
Firework Display !
Spectacular Set Pieces :: Humorous Features
CONCLUDING WITH
THE ERUPTION OF MOUNT ETNA.
Sylvan Illumination.

Flower-bedecked participants of that Floral and River Fête of 1938. The building behind the girls is the old Holy Trinity School, built in 1853, alongside the main road above the river. This is now privately owned and today's children attend a more modern school close to Holy Trinity church on Clifton Road.

Trinity Church, Matlock.

The first subscription towards building Holy Trinity church was only 10s, but over £2,000 was raised and the church was consecrated in October 1842. Erected on a natural tufa terrace, it could only accommodate a north/south alignment instead of the usual west/east – and the pull-ropes in the tower work seven 'gongs' rather than bells.

Clergymen giving their undivided attention to a group warden and a Geiger counter during a Civil Defence course in 1962. This was the era of the Cold War, when people were even building their own fall-out shelters. With considerable optimism, churchmen were deemed useful points of contact in the event of a disaster.

124

The imposing Woodbank was built by George Lawton, manager of Masson Mill, apparently to flaunt his wealth after being refused permission to build at Cromford. The property subsequently belonged to the Holiday Guild and was known as Cromford Court, then later became headquarters of the New Tribes Mission. Woodbank has recently been converted into flats.

Woodbank gave Lawton a bird's-eye view of the mills where he reigned supreme. At the week-long wedding celebrations of his daughter, May, – the last big event at the Palais Royal – Masson millworkers were ordered to change into suits before going up to toast the newly-weds, there to be monitored by three foremen counting the minutes they were away from their labours.

Paul Harrison's photograph of 1983 puts Masson Mills in their rightful setting by the river. Built by Sir Richard Arkwright 200 years earlier as his showpiece mills, Masson was expanded in the early twentieth century by the English Sewing Company, whose £10,000 project included the landmark red-brick chimney.

Today, Masson Mills is a working textile museum open 363 days a year. Old machinery is back in action, with people on the workforce representing families who worked here for generations. This is the bell that called them to work; its Latin inscription translates as 'Untouched, I remain silent. Knock me and I sing sweetly'.

A line of buildings which faced the mills has gone, including the Rutland Arms and a terrace of brick cottages built to house Arkwright's orphan apprentices. Three houses on Masson Terrace, pictured, later accommodated coachmen employed at Masson House. The three-storey building is thought to have once been the cutting department of the nearby paper mill.

As this car left Matlock Bath around fifty years ago, it passed Glenorchy House, since demolished. This was the birthplace, in 1851, of George Newnes, highly successful publisher of the trail-blazing Tit-Bits and classier titles including Country Life and Strand Magazine. Newnes held a strong affection for Matlock and provided financial backing for the tramway.

Acknowledgements

The author is most grateful for the generosity and interest of all who have contributed towards this publication. In particular, for illustrations and information, the following:

Mrs I. Allen; Ann Andrews, for permissions on behalf of the heirs of Mr Frank Clay; Ken Askew; Pat Barnes; the late H.D. Bowtell; A. Broome; Brenda Clarkson; Gordon Coupe; Caroline Dale-Leech; Derbyshire Times; Doncaster Museum and Art Gallery; the Ron Duggins Collection; Beryl Edmonds; Robin Farmer; David Fearn; Mrs A. Harper; Paul Harrison; the late W.P. Head; Fred Hole; Anthony Holmes; Nelly Holmes; Bill Hudson; Mrs D. Hursthouse; Lewis Jackson; the Johnson Collection at Derbyshire Libraries and Heritage Department; Judy Jones; Mrs M. Kaye; Richard Litchfield; Matlock Civic Association; Matlock Fire and Rescue Service; Matlock Mercury; Brian Newton; John Odell at Matlock Golf Club; Peak District Mining Museum; John Phillips and Peak Rail; the Red Cross; Frank Rodgers MBE; R.E. Shaw; Mr and Mrs George Statham; C.R. Taylor; Mrs L. Taylor; John A. Thornley; the Revd Canon John Tomlinson; Beverley Toone; Anne Trinder; Lynn Willies; F. Winfield; and Derek at Tinker Wrights.

Stereoscopic cards were kindly loaned by John Bradley of Ashover, Honorary Curator of The Stereoscopic Society.

Once more, I am deeply indebted to the unflagging and ever-willing assistance of Ruth Gordon and the staff of Derbyshire Libraries and Heritage Department, County Hall.

The southerly route into the Matlocks took a long, roundabout course before a new road was made through the Derwent Valley around 1815. Matlock Bath had previously been separated from Cromford by this steep cliff at Scarthin Nick, but the narrow entrance was blasted open and Matlock Bath never looked back.